Tracy + Marc-

Remember - never buy a VCR on the street in Times Square; and you simply can't win at "3 Card Monte."

Have a great life together!

Brian Cooke

ANTONY SHUGAAR

New York

THE CITY THAT NEVER SLEEPS

This book is dedicated to my father, Carl, and to Elizabeth.

SMITHMARK

N EW YORK

CONTENTS

Text
Antony Shugaar

Graphic design by
Patrizia Balocco

© 1994 Edizioni White Star
Via Candido Sassone, 24
13100 Vercelli, Italy

This edition distributed in the U.S.A. and Canada by SMITHMARK Publishers Inc; 16 East 32nd Street , New York, NY 10016
Tel. (212) 532-6600.

SMITHMARK books are available for bulk purchase for sales promotion and premium use. For details write or call the Manager of Special Sales, SMITHMARK Publishers Inc., 16 East 32nd Street, New York, NY 10016; (212) 532-6600

0-8317-6256-X

Printed in Italy by GEP, Cremona.

1 The Empire State Building, no longer the world's tallest building but still the classical image of a skyscraper, has probably suffered the most gruelling and unforgiving testing of any structure in New York.

2-3 At the southern tip of the island of Manhattan, where heavy guns once surveyed arriving ships, stands Wall Street, a citadel of financial power, glowing in the red sunset.

4-5 Spanning the East River, the second bridge to link Brooklyn with Manhattan is Manhattan Bridge. Farther south, one can just see the glittering cables and dark, ominous piers of the Brooklyn Bridge, completed just over a century ago.

6-7 Overlooking Central Park are some of the wealthiest and most exclusive addresses in the world, those on Fifth Avenue above Fifty-Ninth Street. The park offers the only real assurance available to apartment dwellers in New York that there will never be a taller building across the way, stealing oxygen, sunlight, and the spectacular view.

8 The twin towers of the World Trade Center, with the World Financial Center, glow orange in the sunset. The two colossal skyscrapers, which loom up one hundred and ten stories, were built between 1962 and 1977.

9 Liberty gazes sternly out over New York harbor. The statue was a gift of the French people, while the stone pedestal was the result of a fund-raising drive by Joseph Pulitzer's tabloid daily, the New York World.

INTRODUCTION

New York City, one is tempted to say, needs no introduction. Long identified in the popular imagination as the world's greatest city, there are really three New Yorks, one bigger than the other: the island of Manhattan (2 million people), the five boroughs of New York (Manhattan, Brooklyn, the Bronx, Queens, and Staten Island, 8 million), and Greater New York, which includes broad swaths of New Jersey, to the south (17 million). There are more people in Greater New York than in all of New York State — thus, the Mayor of New York City and the governor of New York state vie in importance. In "Superman," which can safely be called the Great American comic book, New York City is called Metropolis (for rival superhero, Batman, it was Gotham City). To America in the Thirties, and to the whole world ever since, New York City

was the Metropolis, by definition. New York is a city that invites superlatives. Though the first skyscrapers may have been built in Chicago, New York City — specifically, Manhattan Island — established the skyscraper as artform, as skyline, as the "tallest building in the world." The first "tallest building in the world" to be touted as such was the Woolworth Building, built in 1913. The story of its planning and construction may fairly epitomize the New York spirit. The builder was a former haberdasher's clerk named Louis Horowitz, who parlayed the construction of a few apartment buildings into a mighty contracting business, the Thompson-Starrett Co., employing thousands to build the giant towers that began to spring up on Manhattan. As the planning phase for the Woolworth Building came to a close, Horowitz sat down with his client. "Everything checks out, Mr. Woolworth," he said. "The only thing I can't figure out is this: you will be losing money on this building. It doesn't add up." "No," responded Woolworth, founder of America's largest chain of discount stores. "What you don't understand is this. The Woolworth Building will be the world's largest billboard."So it was, and so was the next "tallest building in the world," the Empire State Building — a billboard for a

10-11 A monument to the crass materialism of the Fifties, the sly vulgarity of the Sixties, the urban decay of the Seventies, and the wretched excess of the Eighties, Times Square epitomizes all that is flashy, ostentatious, and violent, tawdry, lavish, and luxurious about New York.

NEW YORK

12-13 Skating, whether on rollerblades or on ice, is one of the city's most popular athletic activities, and Central Park provides a perfect venue for those who love to skate.

movie named "King Kong." New York City is a city of enormous, bustling energy, rising upwards in the skyscrapers that claw at the sky. It is a city that proclaims itself endlessly, advertising its stunning success to the world. It is also a city of outsiders, trusting in luck and inspiration to make them citizens of the world's greatest metropolis. Frank Sinatra sang, "If I can make it there, I'd make it anywhere." E.B. White, in his classic "Here is New York," put it best, however: "On any person who desires such queer prizes, New York will bestow the gift of loneliness and the gift of privacy. It is this largess that accounts for the presence within the city's wall of a considerable section of the population; for the residents of Manhattan are to a large extent strangers who have pulled up stakes somewhere and come to town, seeking sanctuary or fulfillment or some greater or lesser grail. The capacity to make such dubious gifts is a mysterious quality of New York. It can destroy an individual, or it can fulfill him, depending a good deal on luck. No one should come to New York to live unless he is willing to be lucky." Perhaps the finest example of New York rewarding those daring to be lucky is the following: A Navy sailor, during World War II, had a date to meet a girl at one the two lions — popularly known as Leo Astor and Leo Lenox — that guard the entrance to the public library at Forty-Second Street and Fifth Avenue. The sailor suddenly had to ship out, and had no way of breaking his date. He sent her a telegram, care of the North Lion, Public Library, 42nd & 5th, New York City. His luck — and the amazing city that is New York — worked. The telegram was delivered. That is New York City — and then there is the city's physical presence. Manhattan, the heart of New York, is a long narrow island, thirteen miles north to south, bristling with over a hundred skyscrapers, and linked, via six of the world's great bridges and two mighty tunnels, to the mainland. New York is a city that is entirely surrounded by water and is made beautiful by the ocean light and air. Because New York is a tough, hard-charging "city that doesn't sleep," it can sometimes appear harsh,

14 top An aerial view from high above Brooklyn of the Wall Street district, and the structure and Manhattan ramps of the Brooklyn Bridge; in the distance one can see the Manhattan Bridge. The Brooklyn Bridge was built between 1869 and 1883 by J. A. Roebling and by his son, W. A. Roebling.

14 bottom The equestrian statue of General William Tecumseh Sherman, the work of the sculptor Augustus Saint-Gaudens, adorns the southeast corner of Central Park, across from the Plaza Hotel.

violent, even brutal. New Yorkers pride themselves on the city's rough carelessness. Like Texans boasting about their huge rolling ranches, New Yorkers boast of the rudeness of their taxi drivers, their beat cops, their waitresses and short-order cooks. This harsh rudeness is part of a warm, gritty bond that unites the entire city. Wastelands of warehouses and factories, the broken-down waterfronts, the darkest ghettoes and grimiest industrial molochs - all these are part of New York as much as the finest hanging gardens of Sutton Place or the quaintest courts of Greenwich Village. One noted poet raised on the Brooklyn waterfront put it nicely: "Walt Whitman, a kosmos, of Manhattan the son,/Turbulent, fleshy, sensual, eating, drinking/and breeding." New York, with this spirit, has created much of what we consider to be the modern world. This book offers you a tour of what makes up New York. In these pages, the splendid photographic essays are accompanied by a psychic history of the city, with thumbnail portraits of the city's characters, wiseguys, aristocrats, and folk heroes. You will read about a retired naval commander who set out on a personal crusade to walk in every street, avenue, alley, square and court on Manhattan island. You will read about Theodore Roosevelt's tenure as police commissioner of this city when crime was just beginning to raise its organized head. You will read the history of neighborhoods, great hotels, mighty bridges, and towering skyscrapers. You will see the city by night, or covered by a blanket of snow in wintertime, when crosscountry skiers can be seen in Central Park. To describe and chronicle in some way this restless, changable city of many millions is a difficult task. As the introduction to the WPA Guide put it: "the problem of keeping pace, in print, with a dynamic metropolis that overnight replaces a century-old institution with a new triumph in modernity." And in this unstable amalgam of eight million human stories, this naked city, it makes sense only to describe the one thing that remains stable, that cannot be torn down to build a skyscraper; again, quoting from the WPA Guide: "the human character of the city." We hope that the reader will fall in love with this portrait of New York, just as we have fallen in love with the city that doesn't sleep.

15 This remarkable view of the steel and stone features that make up the Brooklyn Bridge show nineteenth-century engineering at its finest. The huge, braided-steel cables grip the steel-and-concrete roadway, balancing it high above the waters of the East River, far below; the artistic outlook of the last century persuaded the engineers to give each pier two very Gothic arches, more typical of a cathedral than a bridge.

16 Flanked by a double procession of skyscrapers, Forty-second Street is dominated by the unmistakable and effortlessly graceful shaft of the Chrysler Building, made still more spectacular by its nighttime lighting.

17 The spectacular Art Deco architecture of a building on Fifth Avenue clashes with the simple lines of the surrounding modern skyscrapers.

18-19 A huge bronze figure of Prometheus, by the sculptor Paul Manship, dominates the sunken plaza in the heart of Rockefeller Center. The plaza is used as an outdoor café in the summertime and as an ice-skating rink in the winter.

20-21 Looking at Manhattan's Wall Street district, and the Battery, one has the impression of a heavily overladen ship, and indeed the weight of concrete, stone, and steel would sink anything less solidly buttressed than the island of Manhattan, built on a foundation of granite.

22-23 Perhaps the time will come when skyscrapers are obsolete, but till that day, this brightly lit metropolis by night is the incarnation and image of modernity. When filmmakers try to convey the pure abstraction of form that is cyberspace, they inevitably use something resembling these glass-and-steel gorges of light and height.

PORTRAIT
OF NEW YORK

The Naked City, it has been called. Certainly, if we consider Manhattan as the heart of it, it is one of the few cities in the world that can be so thoroughly scrutinized. It is a "tight little island," a dozen miles north to south, three and a half across at its widest, and nearly a quarter mile tall at its heart and at the foot of the island, where skyscrapers tower, swaying slightly in the wind.
To appreciate Manhattan at its best, you must leave the island for a moment. From the Brooklyn waterfront — and even better, from high atop any of three of the bridges that span the East River: the Brooklyn, the Williamsburg, and the Fifty-Ninth Street bridges — the tall, narrow island shows to its best advantage. Walking or cycling across those bridges gives a better idea of the city's (and in the city of New York, made up of five separate boroughs, only one borough can safely be referred to as The City — Manhattan) true, amazing nature. All those who live in Manhattan at some point refer with disdain to Brooklynites, Bronxers, Queensians, Staten Islanders, and New Jerseyans, as the "bridge-and-tunnel crowd." To reach the mythical kingdom of Manhattan, these lesser mortals must cross a bridge or go through a tunnel — hence, they are hopelessly provincial, unhip, and pitiable. And yet it is they — the bridge-and-tunnel crowd — that give Manhattan its saving grace, its humility, its human touch. And this is what they see when crossing any of the three most interesting bridges: Cross the Brooklyn Bridge, especially in the glittering half-light of dusk, and you will experience a rare melting of every heart-wrenching cliché of Romantic culture and of modernist culture. What stands before you springs direct from the imaginations of Piranesi and Anaïs Nin; a dizzying canyon of architectural forms, looming black into the evanescent crepuscular light and emphasizing its inconceivable vastness and depth with the occasional hard white fluorescent window, perhaps silhouetting a

24 Wall Street, one of the world's financial capitals, overlooks the East River and the teeming city of Brooklyn on the opposite shore. In this photograph, one can see the Brooklyn Bridge on the left and, beyond it, the Manhattan Bridge.

25 This aerial view of the clustered skyscrapers of Wall Street includes — looking south, at the top right — a tiny patch of green leaves in Battery Park. One can see the distinctively irregular street grid of Wall Street, with doglegs, deadends, and odd angles everywhere, contrasting sharply with the grid of the rest of the island.

N *New York*

26 top Made up of more than a hundred skyscrapers, the New York skyline seems like an enormous stage-set made of concrete and glass, dominating a megalopolis of nearly ten million people.

26-27 Looming at dizzying heights, a number of terraces on New York skyscrapers are equipped with solariums, swimming pools, and tennis courts, to help make up for the haste and crowding of New York City.

27 top Finished in March 1931, the Empire State Building remained the world's tallest building until the late Seventies.

figure looking outward...These are the skyscrapers of lower Manhattan. Beneath you, before you, behind you, and above you is the Brooklyn Bridge itself, with its classic, Gothic arches and brown brick.

One interesting twist on this view can be taken by looking at the series of five photographs by Joshua H. Beal. The photographs show the same view of Lower Manhattan from atop one of the new piers of the Brooklyn Bridge in 1876, before the cables were strung.

The photographs give an astonishing view of a radically different city, though unmistakably New York. It is an odd trick of the mind - when one looks at very old photographs of a city that one knows well, it somehow comes naturally to think of the city as one knows it as somehow, inexplicably, developing into this other city. "Look," one thinks, "Trinity Church was still there," and not, as would be more accurate, "Look, Trinity Church was already there." One thinks of a city as inevitable, already decided, and not of a city that has not yet been decided, that could develop any which-way. Indeed, there is a shock of recognition mixed with bewilderment.

The island recedes southwestward, tapering to the narrow tip of the Battery. Some features are familiar - the sweep of the riverbank, bristling with piers; the narrow dark steeple of Trinity Church; the bell-shaped, almost bulging mansard roofs on the taller buildings (say, fifteen stories), roofs done in the Parisian style, still common below 23rd Street; stricter, chateau-pitched mansards; and red-brick buildings with white window-cornices.

Just as it all begins to seem a bit familiar, one begins to notice that virtually none of these buildings stand taller than five or six stories; an occasional giant rears up fifteen floors. And then there is the dockside, splendid with proud-masted sailing vessels, about a dozen of them, as well as a steam ferry, recognizable as such, and a paddle-wheeled steamer called the Continental, tied up at the wharf of the New Haven Lines. Out to sea, in what are called the roads, stand another fifteen seagoing barks.

To compare this antique view with the same scene as it stands today — dizzying canyons of steel and glass — is to see a relatively ordinary city in its youth and later, in its freakish, overgrown maturity. The Brooklyn Bridge and its close neighbor, the Manhattan Bridge, are graceful, almost diminutive structures compared to the rude strength of the Williamsburg Bridge, which crosses the East River about a mile further north.

The Williamsburg Bridge, completed around the turn of the century, is a mightier piece of work. Perhaps the following is a perfect thumbnail portrait of the bridge — recently, crossing the Williamsburg Bridge by bicycle, one could look down to one's left and see the slowly budging lanes of automobile and truck traffic; to the right, subways rattled along the tracks cut through the bridge's center; overhead, above the cast-iron dedication listing civic leaders and engineers, now overswarmed by graffiti, and above the neo-Egyptian iron piers, soared a sea-plane, still dripping from its East River takeoff. Helicopters touched down at the heliport, a mile or so to the north, while a big, rusty freighter lay moored at the Domino sugar factory in the bridge's shadow on the Brooklyn shore. A temple, in short, to modern transportation.

And then, some seventy blocks north, the Fifty-Ninth Street Bridge. This is a twentieth-century bridge, towering hundreds of feet above the water, offering a view with sweep and dimension. Inland, due west, looms the wedge-crowned Citibank Building with its frequent head-dress of trailing mist. To the south are the other great skyscrapers of mid-town Manhattan: the Chrysler Building, the former Pan Am Building (now emblazoned "MetLife"), the Empire State Building, and far off in the distance, the twin towers of the World Trade Center. Along the northern side of the bridge runs a cable-car line; the great ungainly gondolas sliding along at road level and then dropping down to Roosevelt Island beneath. To the east stands the only true skyscraper in all of Queens, the most suburban borough of the five — the

28-29 Perhaps the best known piece of sculpture in America, the one hundred fifty-one-foot-tall statue of "Liberty Enlightening the World," by Frédéric Auguste Bartholdi, overlooks New York harbor from atop a granite-and-concrete pedestal itself one

hundred and forty-two feet high. The inner structure of the statue was designed by Alexandre Gustave Eiffel, who also built the tower that bears his name. The statue portrays a woman stepping from broken shackles, her uplifted right hand holding a burning torch, while in her left hand is the Declaration of Independence, dated "July 4, 1776."

30-31 The luxurious
apartment towers lining
Central Park West are
reflected in the still waters of
the Central Park Reservoir.

Citicorp Building, rearing hundreds of feet amidst squat row houses, warehouses, and store fronts. And, looking down onto the Manhattan shoreline, a careful study reveals a splendid vignette of New York at its intricate best, a perfect juxtaposition of the clustering masses and the privileged few. This is a famous stretch of shoreline, with the FDR Drive running along the water's edge in an immense concrete gallery. The gaze rises from the river's flow, to the roaring strip of automobiles charging northward, and upward still to the amazing hanging gardens and terraces built atop the concrete abutments lining the highway. Look even more carefully, and you will be able to make out Beekman Place and Sutton Place, two of the most elegant and expensive mini-neighborhoods in the city. Beekman Place in particular is a spectacularly intricate castle-like pile of brownstone high-rise apartments, dotted with terraces, set-backs, and balconies; where the street ends above the river's edge, a tortuous series of stairways winds down to the handkerchief of green shaded park that has cunningly been cut out, amidst patches of green pocket-gardens. And, most spectacular of all, one fortunate city-dweller has a gorgeous garden, in the English style, that simply spreads out over a good hundred square feet of the covered highway. Such is the view from the Fifty-Ninth Street bridge. The George Washington Bridge spans the mighty Hudson above Harlem, connecting New Jersey with the northern tip of Manhattan. From here, the island seems like an orderly cliffside of apartments, more like a particularly dramatic pueblo than a real city.
To the northeast nestles The Cloisters, a genuine piece of medieval architecture purchased in Europe, dismantled in the most businesslike fashion, and shipped across the Atlantic, like so much of the city's remarkable artistic heritage. And so, in this burrow or labyrinth of New York, that is the view from outside.

32 The planners of Central Park hoped simply to create a giant touchstone of rural goodness and calming greenery in the heart of what even then was the most advanced and engineering-oriented of cities.

33 In this spectacular aerial view, showing Manhattan as seen from the Battery, the island seems like an immense ship anchored to the mainland by two suspension bridges, like giant moorings.

34-35 An aerial view from high above Brooklyn of the Wall Street district, and the structure and Manhattan ramps of the Brooklyn Bridge. South Street Seaport, with its tall-masted ships, can be seen to the left of the bridge.

36-37 Jostling for position, the skyscrapers of New York are the perfect metaphor for the competitive capitalists that inhabit them. Each skyscraper is designed to concentrate all its identity in its peak, summit, or top-knot. Here is the distinctive MetLife building, which started life as the Pan Am building. With the demise of the airline, the building was — figuratively — scalped, and a new name made its appearance. In the distance is the distinctive wedge cap of the Citibank Building, and to the right is the lovely Deco chrome of the Chrysler Building.

38-39 Fifth Avenue and the Avenue of the Americas, made even more visible by the light trails of nighttime traffic, seem to trace glowing lines toward the World Trade Center and Battery Park; at the bottom, on the left, one can clearly see the peak of the Metropolitan Life Tower, a skyscraper built in 1909, and modelled after the bell tower of Saint Mark's, in Venice.

SKYSCRAPERS

These stories, and the buildings in which they occur, since the beginning of the century, have been stacked ever higher in the sky of New York. Manhattan is blessed with a particularly tough rocky foundation, and there have been practically no limits on the height of the buildings. It is interesting to read the words of a figure straight out of Edith Wharton's "The Age of Innocence," named Deems Taylor, prophesying, in 1928, the future of a New York covered with skyscrapers. His pamphlet is entitled, "The city that died of greatness", He wrote, "Around Grand Central Station, in a district less than 200 yards square, stands — or will stand, shortly — a group of skyscrapers whose floor space totals nearly 100 acres and whose tenants outnumber the combined populations of Cheyenne, Wyoming; Brownsville, Texas; Reno, Nevada; Emporia, Kansas; and Albuquerque, New Mexico, some 65,000 souls. Just what is going to happen when all these new congeries discharge their inmates upon streets already stuffed like a Strassbourg goose is a question that has at last caused a certain amount of uneasiness in high circles. As one of a handful of New Yorkers who were actually born in the city, I remember New York when it had no skyscrapers; when the steeple of Trinity Church and the gilded dome of the Pulitzer Building were two towering landmarks on the skyline". An apocalyptic vision of the future of New York — of the city, after all, that served as the model for the nightmarish pinnacles of the Gotham City of "Batman". Certainly, the skyscrapers have made New York what it is, every one of them — the hyper-Gothic splendor of the Woolworth Building, the Art Deco splendor of the Chrysler Building, the sheer power of the Empire State Building, the weird Chippendale baroque of the postmodern AT&T Building, the odd wedge-shaped cap of the Citicorp Building, the twin towers of the World Trade Center — endowing the city's skyline with yet another tile in the mosaic of its personality. Every new skyscraper, in fact, has been accompanied by new cries of gloom and doom, so much so that one almost suspects at this point that architectural critics and public officials have

40 As glass and steel "skins" have come to replace the stone and brick of earlier times, the architect's job has become a delicate one: they must respect the economics of vast, unbroken sameness, and still introduce some element of identity. Here, in the U.N. Plaza, the goal has been achieved with contours and shaping of the skyscraper's geometric shape.

41 The Empire State Building, 1,250 feet high, is a great limestone-and-steel lighthouse in the heart of Manhattan, and, it has been said, a monument to an epoch: the boom years of the late Twenties. Atop the shaft, at the eighty-sixth-floor level, is the two-hundred-foot observation tower, an inverted test-tube shape buttressed by great flaring corner piers.

42 top The complex of the United Nations Buildings is formed of four buildings designed by W. Harrison and M. Abramovitz; a number of other architects from all over the world worked on them as well, including Le Corbusier and Oscar Niemeyer.

come to enjoy the ritual. There were gloomy forebodings upon the construction of the outsized twin towers of the World Trade Center, there was anguished esthetic breast-beating at the completion of the admittedly garish and luxurious Trump Tower, and now that plans are going forward for a giant new skyscraper complex on the West Side, New York media and politicians are gnashing their teeth and rending their garments over this one, too. The fact is that each ambitious new scheme proves to be an advertisement of the city's greatness. Each time, the city finds a way of dealing with the various problems created. New York invented the skyscraper, then New York invented setbacks, which are recessions of the upper part of the building, designed to reduce the structure's weight, and to permit light and air to penetrate to street level and to the lower floors. With each new generation of skyscraper, the city has invented a new set of civilizing conditions upon the towering structures. And each new generation of skyscraper sets New York apart. Not only are New York skyscrapers the cunningly crafted products of the concerted efforts of hundreds of skilled craftsmen, engineers, designers, and decorators. In addition to having the populations of small towns, they have all the amenities. There are many different sorts of eating places in a skyscraper, for example. Although not all of it was built, the gem of skyscraper interior decoration can be found in the plans for the Chrysler Building, by William Van Allen. They called for several gymnasiums, an observation lounge, an automobile salon, a Renaissance-style duplex apartment for Walter Chrysler himself, and the nicely named Cloud Club. New York has built over a hundred skyscrapers, and New York will continue to do so, because the skyscraper is so good at what it does.
A skyscraper is a giant organizational chart in the city skies, a map of power, privilege, and luxury, where the geographic compass points straight up. The crown of creation, of course, is the roof garden, although some roof gardens, very high up, can be like sitting on the wing of a plane. The chief attraction of a Manhattan skyscraper roof garden is the view: literally hundreds of city blocks stretch out in every direction, endlessly interesting by day, black velvet and glittering light by night.

42-43 The product of an earlier time, the Chrysler Building seems to be a hymn in steel and stone. This was one of the first skyscrapers to use exposed metal as an integral part of its design.

43 right The early light of morning spreads through the canyons of skyscrapers, transforming the materials of the facades into a warm golden glow.

44 A quarter of a million people enter and leave the twin towers of the World Trade Center every day, while there are fifty thousands full time employees who work here. These colossal structures, 1,348 feet tall, were designed by the Japanese architect, Minoru Yamazaki.

45 The Chrysler Building has been one of the most glorious symbols of New York since 1930.

47 top The unmistakable shape of the Citibank Building rises to a height of nine hundred and fifteen feet over Manhattan: this steel, aluminum, and glass giant stands on pylons one hundred thirty-foot-tall, which have made it possible to create substantial public spaces at the foot of the skyscraper.

46 top Although it is dwarfed by the bulk of the MetLife Building, the Helmsley Building has itself become a familiar landmark to New Yorkers.

46 bottom In line with the latest architectural trends, such as the postmodern style, New York's skyline has become even more interesting and varied.

46-47 New York is a blend of extremely varied architectural styles, often in sharp and clashing contrast; but, even with the revolution in tastes over the last few decades many of the skyscrapers built in the first half of the century still look modern.

48-49 With all the exuberance that so distinguishes his work, Donald Trump has chosen to adorn the already fairly forlorn trees in the hanging gardens of Trump Tower with a garish array of Christmas lights. The result is quite fascinating.

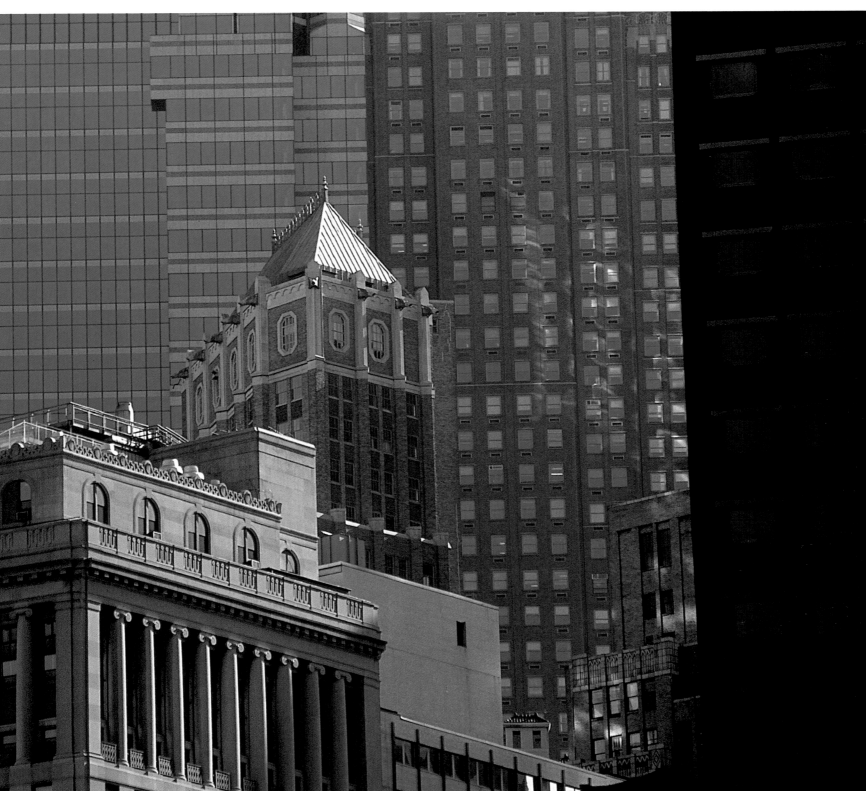

50 top A view of the spire of St. Paul's Chapel, the oldest church in Manhattan, and probably the only building that presents its back to Broadway. Set amidst the imposing silhouettes of modern skyscrapers, this church was once attended by George Washington, who came here to pray even before the Revolutionary War.

50 bottom The light-blue roof of this structure contains all of the Gothic vernacular found in early skyscrapers, considered to be "Cathedrals of Commerce."

51 This onion-dome cupola of a synagogue on Lexington Avenue represents the city's vast Jewish population, which largely immigrated from Europe and Russia during the century from 1850 to 1950.

52-53 A view from New Jersey of the World Trade Center and World Financial Center at sunset. The entire southern tip of the island of Manhattan glows orange in the last rays of sunshine, with a special luminosity given by the presence of the wide waters of the Hudson River.

54-55 The foot of the twin towers of the World Trade Center and the shorter World Financial Center glow in the last rays of sunset. The boats that cluster at the foot of these modern citadels, which are already strangely reminiscent of medieval architecture, give a further sense of fortification.

56 The remarkable angles
and planes of this recent
skyscraper show the
conceptualist influence of
architect I.M. Pei. The glass-
and-steel "skin" approach to
skyscraper design allows an
esthetic of almost pure
mathematics, in a Cubist
sensibility.

57 A sort of Abstract
Expressionist twist is given to
New York's architecture in
this funhouse-mirror-like
view of the St. Paul's Chapel,
reflected in the windows of
the oddly-spelled Millenium
Hotel.

LIFE IN THE STREETS

So much for Manhattan's exterior. A newspaper article that appeared in The New York Times in 1954 offers a perfect sequel into the matter of Manhattan's streets and neighborhoods. The article, by a Pulitzer prize-winning observer of New York, Meyer Berger, reported: "Men sometimes set themselves to curious objectives. Commander Thomas J. Keane, 65 years old today, hopes to complete next Sunday afternoon, if the weather is bright, a project that he started a little less than four years ago - to walk in every street, avenue, alley, square and court on Manhattan island." "He intends to start from the northern end of Broadway on Marble Hill around 1 o'clock in the afternoon and do the thirteen miles to the Battery. That will complete his self-imposed task. He thinks that at his normal walking pace, three and one-half miles an hour,

he should make it within four hours."
The officer, Berger reported, was a short, brisk blue-eyed man with remarkably good color. He had started his walk at the island's southern tip, taking all east-west streets. He had had to weave and backtrack a lot in the crooked lanes and alleys of the Financial District and in Greenwich Village. Proceeding northward, he had worked the flanks of Central Park as solid east and west blocks — he then resumed river-to-river hikes north of 110th Street. In all, in so doing, Commander Keane covered 3,022 city blocks, a distance of about 502 miles. After walking all the side streets, he covered the avenues, working from east to west. Broadway was chosen to be last because it is the only road that runs the island's full thirteen miles of length.
For all the ground that he covered, Keane had a relatively slim body of adventures to report. Perhaps the most intriguing things he reported were that, in the early 1950s, there had been a goat farm at 128th Street, near the East River, and that there were shacks on stilts on the Harlem River, at the island's northernmost tip, off the Bronx shoreline. These are streets that have seen a remarkable series of personalities; the same sidewalks have been pounded by Abraham Lincoln and Andy Warhol; the same subway gratings have supported the

58 Fifth Avenue is the stomping ground of wealthy New Yorkers almost by definition, and where there are wealthy New Yorkers, there are yellow cabs in droves. Veiled by a melancholy film of rain, the street loses a bit of its frigid composure, and acquires a more human dimension.

59 This photograph shows Fifth Avenue with a number of its iconic signifiers: flags, stoplights, discreetly glowing display windows, taxis, buses, bare wet trees, and — above all — skyscrapers.

N New York

60 top Cabs cruise uptown along Sixth Avenue, reflected in the mirror-like glass ceiling of the International Promenade Lounge of the New York Hilton and Towers.

60-61 This Checker cab is an anachronism from an earlier decade: out of the tens of thousands of yellow cabs in New York, only a dozen or so are still Checkers. Too bad: they were the most comfortable taxi cabs in America.

61 top The New York taxicab constitutes a fundamental part of the public transportation network. In order to operate one, the driver or owner must purchase a medallion, which costs as much as a fair-sized house in the suburbs.

weight of Marilyn Monroe and Albert Einstein; the same narrow Wall Street canyons have showered down ticker tape upon returning veterans from World War II, triumphant astronauts, rescued hostages, and the surprised and relieved vets of the short war in the Persian Gulf. One particularly evocative image of New York's streets is that given by Theodore Roosevelt in a series of letters to his sister. Roosevelt was serving as a police commissioner, and striving unsuccessfully to reform the city's police force.

One letter, dated 19 May 1895, said, "I have never worked harder than during the last two weeks... I shall speedily assail some of the ablest, shrewdest men in the city, who will be fighting for their lives... Yet in spite of the nervous strain and worry, I am glad I undertook it; for it is a man's work." A month later, Roosevelt reported: "Twice I have spent the night in patrolling New York on my own account, to see exactly what the men were doing... The trips did good, though each meant going forty hours at a stretch without any sleep." And a week after that, he wrote: "I make some startling discoveries at times. These midnight rambles are great fun... I get a glimpse of the real life of the city's swarming millions." The picture of a sleep-deprived Teddy Roosevelt walking the midnight streets of Manhattan, eyewitness to the endless parade of streetlife and crime, transcends time, and becomes emblematic of the city's sleepless, late-night walkers, adventurers in an unparalleled dreamscape. Manhattan remained all too real in its pragmatic corruption, however. In February 1896, Roosevelt admitted to his sister that his reform drive had failed, adding bitterly: "Public sentiment is apathetic and likes to talk about virtue in the abstract, but it does not want to obtain the virtue if there is any trouble about it." If these streets are endless conduits pounded by beat-cops, theater-goers, retired naval captains, and all of life's rich parade, they are also the setting for some of the most valuable real estate in the world. The names that attach to the real estate are themselves legend and epic. Take the corner of 34th Street and Fifth Avenue. One old photograph shows this corner in 1898. A modest, four-story

62 It is interesting to note the way in which the skyscrapers of the 1910s — clearly symbols of a new era — incorporated a remarkable mix of revolutionary technology and architectural styles belonging to the past; in particular, New York architects showed a real weakness for the Neo-Classical and all its decorative motifs.

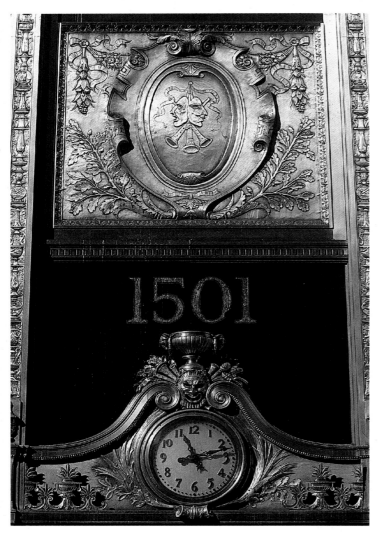

63 Ice skaters rattle and pirouette over the surface of the sunken plaza of Rockefeller Center's Channel, under the golden warmth and benevolent gaze of Prometheus, bringer of fire to mankind.

64-65 Bicyclists leaving Manhattan via the Brooklyn Bridge. The climb to this central section of the bridge is painful, but the view from up there is well worth the effort.

66-67 Along its length, Park Avenue ranges from a street of industrial brawn and bustling commerce (the southern half) to a stiff-lipped boulevard of powerfully respectable and eminently residential buildings (to the north). In both incarnations, however, Park Avenue maintains its characteristic divider island.

68-69 The Fifth Avenue entrance to Rockefeller Center's International Building features an uncommonly fine piece of proportion between a statue — Atlas, apparently bearing Science and Industry on his shoulders — and the surrounding architecture.

brownstone stood on the corner, then, the home of the redoubtable Mrs. Astor, queen of New York's society. Toward the rear of the building falls a dark and ominous shadow. The shadow was cast by the Waldorf Hotel, which her nephew, William Waldorf Astor, had erected as an act of vengeance upon his aunt, from whom his wife had been unable to wrest the leadership of New York society. "Less than a year after it was completed," writes John Kouwenhoven, a New York historian, "Mrs. Astor capitulated and hired the architect Richard Morris Hunt to build her new house uptown. In 1897, her son erected the Astoria on the old site, and the combined hotels were operated as a unit to the profit of both the rival branches of the family." The huge and stately Waldorf Astoria moved uptown to its present full-block location at 49th Street and Lexington Avenue in the early Thirties. The site at the corner of 34th and Fifth, once occupied by Mrs. Astor's unpretentious brownstone, is now the location of the Empire State Building. Another lost denizen of New York's midtown speaks volumes about the city's flora and fauna, the city's "human character." Again, Meyer Berger reported in the 11 August 1954 edition of The New York Times, on the closing of the Fifth Avenue Bank, on the northwest corner of 44th Street. "No other bank in the city caters to so many dowagers," Berger reported, "ladies who were Avenue belles sixty and seventy years ago. No other bank building has retained so warmly the social and physical flavor of the Eighties and Nineties." Many of the bank's employees had worked there for fifty years or more, Berger noted. "The men in the vaults know better than to lift an eyebrow when some quivery-fingered lady paws over her wig collection in the safe deposit chamber." Apparently, one elderly woman client in Westbury, Long Island, once asked the bank to send her a man with a pistol. One of her stable of hunting horses had broken a leg. Employees remembered Hetty Green, the Witch of Wall Street, Mrs. Andrew Carnegie, Anna Gould de Talleyrand, the Princess Galitzene, and Barbara Hutton as a cute little girl.

70-71 Here are scenes from some of New York's most wonderful shopping areas: the atrium of the Trump Tower; Aquascutum on Fifth Avenue; and Macy's. Macy's, with a floor area of more than 7,405,570 square feet, and more than ten thousand employees, is probably the largest department store in the world.

72-73 This remarkable piece of architectural craftsmanship, dating from the Thirties, is situated in the courtyard of the International Building of Rockefeller Center, on Fifth Avenue.

74-75 The clutter and signage of midtown Manhattan on the West Side is a form to itself. It reaches its highest form in Times Square of course, which is as vulgar and wanton and garish in the same proportion as the newspaper after which it is named is discreet and bland and tasteful.

636 FIFTH AVENUE

76 The exquisitely New York vocation for the spectacular is nicely illustrated by the remarkable decoration of this double-decker bus.

77 top Lincoln Center, with its De Chirico-like architecture and its Alhambra-like reflecting pool, is the beating heart of New York's classical culture. The Metropolitan Opera House is located here, as is the Juilliard School, the leading music school in America.

77 center The statue of George Washington is believed to mark the exact spot upon which the First President stood to take his oath of office in 1789. The monument stands in Wall Street, in front of the Federal Hall Memorial, a building that resembles the Parthenon.

77 bottom New York at its most muscular and industrial is just not what it used to be, as this powder-pink Autocar truck cab demonstrates.

78-79 Battery Park lies at the southern foot of Manhattan Island. The British erected a fortress here in 1693, with a battery of guns that swept the only ocean approach to the island, giving the point its name. Now the park is the piece of greenery closest to Wall Street, where money in serious quantities seems to be the dominant form of greenery.

In 1945, a Miss Inza Stephens Pratt, a client of the bank, sent the bank a card: "Dear Bank," it read, "I just got your calendar, and I just got to thinking. I'll bet nobody ever sends you a Christmas card, personal like. Thanks for being a nice, gracious bank with good taste."

Spy Magazine, until its recent demise one of the great institutions of New York City, established a scientific equation to measure the two qualities most highly prized by New York's dowagers and ex-belles. "You can never," they opine, "be too rich or too thin." Not surprisingly, when Spy published its epochal article — "Too Rich and Too Thin" — with its coefficient of thinness and richness, the leader of the pack was a descendent of the Mrs. Astor whose brownstone once stood at 34th and Fifth — Brooke Astor. If these svelte and elegant ladies who lunch are characteristic of Midtown and the Upper East Side, perhaps we can characterize a number of other Manhattan neighborhoods by their inhabitants. We shall try to offer a brief, partial, guided tour. Let us begin, then, with the tip of Manhattan, working our way upward just far enough to cover no more than a representative sampling.

The southernmost tip is the Battery, now occupied by a park from which the Statue of Liberty can be seen along with the ferryboats chugging to and fro among Staten Island, Ellis Island, and Liberty Island. There have been numerous plans to change the face of Manhattan's southern point. In the end, the decision was made to leave it as a park, but it is interesting to imagine some of the faces the Battery might have assumed. This bizarre addition to New York's skyline would have blocked out the view down the Broadway canyon. Numerous other plans have been advanced and - happily - defeated, and the Battery remains an unadorned piece of parkland, overlooking the shipping roads where graceful eagle-winged sailing ships, and more recently tramp steamers, once brought coffee from Brazil, rubber from Sumatra, and bananas from Costa Rica.

The Wall Street district itself — canyon of skyscrapers, businessmen, and ticker-tape parades — has been

described so often as to make any further account redundant. Numerous historical details however serve to set the stage — the author Washington Irving was born at 131 William Street, at the corner of Fulton Street, an appropriate birthplace, as has been noted, for the man who coined the phrase "the Almighty Dollar."

In this neighborhood, in 1920, a carriage loaded with explosives blew up, killing thirty and wounding hundreds; a terrorist attack of this viciousness was not seen again in the United States until 1993, when the World Trade Center, a few dozen blocks away was rocked by a similar car-bomb, killing six. Pearl Street, in this same neighborhood, maintains its melancholy charm; in about 1691, Captain William Kidd, a pirate legendary for his bloody cruelty, lived here. Maiden Lane is the site of a meandering brook over which ran a little bridge, used by lovers in their trysts; hence the charming name. Further north still is City Hall, where the Brooklyn Bridge touches Manhattan, and the more recent Woolworth Building, known as the Cathedral of Commerce, and the first of the modern skyscrapers for which New York is perhaps most famous.

The Woolworth Building was in principle a gigantic billboard for the chain of five-and-dime stores of the same name; the purpose was achieved, and the building made the stores world-famous. North of the Brooklyn Bridge is Chatham Square, the boundary separating Wall Street and the City Hall area from Chinatown. Once the haunts of such legendary (and predominantly Irish) New York gangs as the Forty Thieves, the Kerryonians, the Chichesters, the Plug Uglies, the Shirt Tails, the Dead Rabbits, and of course the immortal Bowery Boys, bowdlerized into harmlessness in the films of the same name. And here, in the Thirties, were shops such as that of Rocks Grillo, who fixed black eyes, and Charlie Wagner, the "champion tattooing artist of the world." North of here begins the Lower East Side, about which it has been said that "anarchism, communism, and revolution have all been discussed thoroughly in its streets and byways."

80 This statue of George Washington was the work of John Quincy Adams Ward in 1883; on the stairs of Federal Hall, there are always plenty of New Yorkers and tourists sitting and watching the frenzied traffic and street life of Wall Street.

81 The Stock Exchange, temple to what Washington Irving (who was born a few blocks away from here) called "the Almighty Dollar." In this wide-angle view of the New York Stock Exchange (note the initials "NYSE") traders cluster around trading stations and scraps of paper litter the ground, despite the increasing electronization of the deals.

N/EW YORK

82-83 By the time of the First World War, Washington Square was one of the last enclaves for the wealthy of New York and an aristocratic stronghold. The rich and the socially desirable by-and-large abandoned lower Manhattan and moved uptown. Washington Square around this same time became the center of a strange new development in New York life: young, penniless rebel artists. Greenwich Village thus became world famous; nowadays, the entire park is an oasis of peace and fun amidst the frantic New York pace.

This is historically the destination for immigrants of all sorts — in the first half of this century, in particular, Yiddish was as common here as English. Letters to the editor of the Jewish Daily Forward, one of the leading Yiddish newspapers of this part of town, speak volumes about the life that was led here. Some sample openings from the letters section, known as "A Bintel Brief," are given here, translated into English. The fraught, tragic, histrionic nature of these letters tells us much about life in the Lower East Side: (1906) "I hope that you will give me the opportunity to tell the world about my sufferings"; (1906) "I am a Russian revolutionist and a freethinker. Here in America I became acquainted with a girl who is also a freethinker"; (1907) "I am one of those unfortunate girls thrown by fate into a dark and dismal shop, and I need your counsel"; (1908) "I am an unhappy lonely orphan girl, fifteen years of age, and I appeal to you in my helplessness"; (1909) "I am a young man of twenty-two and have every reason to be happy, but I am unhappy because nature saw fit to give me red hair"; (1910) "This is the voice of thirty-seven miserable men who are buried but not covered over by earth, tied down but not in chains, silent but not mute, whose hearts beat like humans, yet are not like other human beings"; (1911) "Please do me a service and print my letter, because in a few days I will no longer be among the living"; (1913) "I am a man who has already lived half his years and I can say that I have never had any peace"; (1933) "I have been a reader of your paper all the nineteen years that I have been in America, and I can tell you that here, in this country, I have not yet had one quiet minute." If this is the spirit of the Lower East Side, compare it with the more luxurious Bohemian spirit of Greenwich Village, exemplified by a bit of doggerel written by a Village poet in the early years of this century: "In the summer I'm a nudist/ In the winter I'm a Buddhist." One could proceed, neighborhood by neighborhood, to cover the vast city, but there would never be an end of tiny communities with powerful, overwrought personalities. New York, the city of eight million different stories.

83 top left Set in Washington Square, the Washington Arch marks the geographic heart of Greenwich Village; this marks the beginning of Fifth Avenue.

83 top right The handsome red-brick Federal row houses lining the north side of Washington Square are some of New York's oldest buildings and the pride of Greenwich Village.

84-85 The New School for Social Research, founded in 1919, is an intellectual touchstone for a certain school of reform-minded. This mural clearly draws some parallels between the work of the subway graffiti and the somewhat subversive scholarship of the New School.

ING "

...K GROWING INTO THE
...S END. OMEGA ALPHA
...BEHZED OSTRS...
...TIII DESTRUCTION
MOTHER EARTH
SCREAMS WITH
THE TEARS
A THOUSAND
SHE DRIPS WIT...
...TION, DROPS OF BLOOD

86 top righ This little shop, on Prince Street, reveals much about the neighborhood — this place is both a neighborhood furniture store and a souvenir shop, as many houses in this section of the Village are actually furnished with souvenirs.

86 center left The Hard Rock Café, on West Fifty-Seventh Street, is exactly what one might imagine it to be: a true temple of rock and roll, where every dish on the menu corresponds to a hit song or a great rock star. This is a hip restaurant, full of autographed photographs and rock souvenirs.

86 center right Across from the Museum of Modern Art, a little sidewalk art stand provides copies of the originals across the street; for a few dollars, one can carry home a Picasso or a Modigliani.

86 bottom right Sheridan Square, near Christopher Street, is socially one of the liveliest places in New York, and these hyperrealistic statues by George Segal represent some of the denizens of the neighborhood.

87 This full-building mural, showing ungainly cows parachuting into an alpine meadow, says much about the absurdist sense of humor that characterizes this section of the West Village, on La Guardia Place between Houston and West Fourth Street.

88 top A sort of Asia in miniature, where Cantonese, emigrants from Hong Kong, Taiwanese, and Vietnamese all live, Chinatown is a clear indication of New York's polyglot nature. On the sidewalk stands and in the crowded little shops, one can find all the ingredients for exotic dishes, along with fans, ivory carvings, and any number of tourist gewgaws.

88-89 This distinctive building at the corner of Canal Street and Centre Street, with the green pagoda roof and red lacquered columns, expresses better than words can do the spirit of Chinatown, a true microcosm of Asia in which the many cultural traditions of many ethnic groups live side by side with the western world.

89 top The active sidewalk markets of Chinatown, along Canal Street, give some idea of the wide array of goods available to discerning shoppers and gawking tourists.

89 bottom Although the newer generations are almost completely americanized, Chinatown maintains its allegiance to ancient cultural heritage, at least externally.

90 Like the Chinese, their next-door neighbors, the Italians of New York, have an active, business-minded little community, and the facades of the buildings tell one and all that business is good and — it's time to eat. Though one will certainly not find New York's finest Italian cooking in Little Italy, the place is great fun. Ristorante Puglia, at 189 Hester Street, proudly proclaims it has been in business for seventy-five years.

91 top left The images that are typical of Little Italy necessarily include the bit of bad taste found in stores selling t-shirts and other articles featuring the Italian flag, as well as historical episodes that may be unlikely, but that are proof of true "Italian-ness."

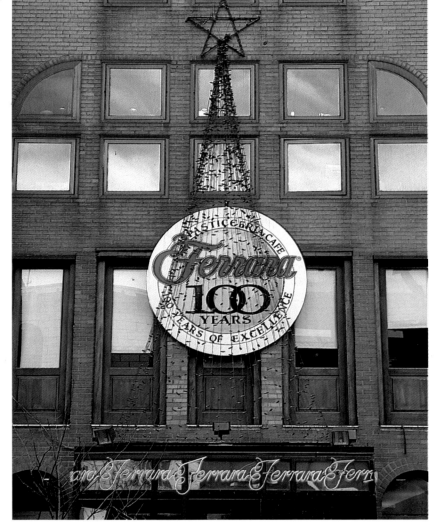

91 top right Ferrara's pastry shop, at 195 Grand Street, has been in business for more than a century: one can get the best coffee in Little Italy here.

91 center left The "Piemonte Ravioli Co.," clearly proud of its Northern Italian roots, is also located on Grand Street.

91 bottom Little Italy is known chiefly for its food stores; nonetheless, the entire neighborhood is redolent with a sense of human warmth, which transcends its business side, making it a place particularly beloved by New Yorkers.

92 Little Italy turns out en masse to celebrate two major feast days, perhaps indicative of the provenance, variously from northern and southern Italy, of its residents. Saint Anthony of Padua, clearly, hails from the north as do his worshippers, while San Gennaro is about as Neapolitan as one can get. Each of the feast days bring huge numbers of people to the narrow streets of Little Italy, turning the neighborhood into a spectacular array of colors.

93 The feast of San Gennaro is celebrated every year, in September; during the feast, Mulberry Street fills up with hundreds of sidewalk stands, featuring Italian delicacies of all sorts. The festivities culminate with a procession, in which the statue of the saint is carried through the street, and offerings of money.

N E W Y O R K

94 left The greenswards of Central Park, the creation of Frederick Law Olmsted, one of America's great natural landscape architects, can be put to all sorts of amusing purposes, including a game of "bocce," or lawn bowling.

94 top The bridges of Central Park, which are among what one author calls "the park's architectural grace notes," were the work of Calvert Vaux, a British professional architect. Each of these bridges boasts a different design, as they are made of many different materials, including brick, stone, and cast iron, a favored material of the day.

94-95 Young couples row to and fro across the Reservoir, while in the background, above the trees, peak the roofs of several of Central Park West's most elegant residences: from left, the Dakota (where "Rosemary's Baby" was filmed, and where John Lennon was shot), the Langham, the San Remo (with its towers), and the Kenilworth.

96-97 A young woman takes her dog for a walk through the splendid morning light in the park; without Central Park, New York would very likely be quite unlivable.

98-99 The East Coast Memorial, at the center of Battery Park, is made up of eight solid sawn-granite monoliths, bearing the names of the merchant mariners who died at sea off the East Coast of the U.S. in World War Two.

95 top Two horse-drawn carriages — institutions in the finest Manhattan tradition — proceed under the leafy shade of the park's roadways.

WINTER IN NEW YORK

Winter in New York is pleasant and enjoyable chiefly in comparison with summer in New York. The seasons that can be considered pleasant in this city are spring and autumn. The spring is gorgeous and — to the degree possible in a city of concrete and steel — green, while the autumn is lovely and crisp and there are no leaves to be raked. The summer, on the other hand, is pretty much like being locked in a giant pressure cooker with your neighbor's stereo; the winter has a few advantages: the pressure cooker moves inside and takes the form of steam heat, and if you are lucky, your landlord will provide it infrequently, and with the windows all closed, the neighbor's stereo is less of a problem. The winter is harsh in New York — but in a way that makes it the most genuinely New Yorkish of seasons. Somehow, bundled in overcoats

scarves, and heavy boots, it is swifter, cooler, and more tragically hip to stride purposefully along the sidewalks of the East Village: more so than dressed in bermuda shorts and polo shirts. Winter in New York is a time of holidays — from Thanksgiving to Christmas, the streets are full of shopping and decorations and giant floats in parades and outsized Christmas trees at Rockefeller Center. It is a time in which the city goes mushmouthed and corny, a time when ice skaters describe parabolas in the park. "Christ came down from His cross today" — according to a poem by Lawrence Ferlinghetti — at the sight of New York's crass commercialism. In the poem, it was the sight of the Rockettes that brought the Savior to point of renouncing His sacrifice; nowadays it might be the sight of FAO Schwartz, where children can purchase outsized electric toy Ferraris and ten-foot-tall teddy bears. There is more to winter than the commercial frenzy of holiday shopping however; more than just the Saabs and Audis with ski racks heading north; more than just the package tours to the islands. For one thing, there is snow. In 1994, New York got hit with one of its toughest winters — seventeen major winter storms piled the snow up so that it seemed never to melt. Infinitely resourceful, the city

100 Fifth Avenue is perhaps the most genteel of New York's shopping and business avenues (Madison Avenue rivals it). Here, the elements show their traditional disregard for the rules of better society: snow, rain, and the bitter arrows of winter cause one and all to raise umbrellas and walk gingerly.

101 The ghostly shape of the Empire State Building looms through the driving snow; it is always curious to see skyscrapers blanketed with snow, even hundreds of feet above the drifts at street level.

N EW YORK

102 top Taxis rush through the city like a chaotic yellow bloodstream, and are shown, ready to surge forward at the signal, on Park Avenue.

102-103 Fifth Avenue, under the assault of a chilly snowfall, loses a great deal of its poise and charm: with a weather like this, an empty taxi is quickly transformed into an island of warmth and comfort.

103 top This misty scene in Times Square is notable for the eerie absence of the usual stream of yellow cabs rushing to deliver their fares or else prowling in search of customers.

104-105 Steam, snow, and auto exhaust give this typical winter street scene that inimitable hellish cast that so distinguishes New York in any season of the year.

106-107 In winter months, Central Park becomes an even more subtle paradox: a patch of forestland moved mysteriously into the heart of the city. The park is lovely, dark, and deep under the snow, but quite often New Yorkers are too busy to enjoy it: yet a few wander through the park or even go cross-country skiing, a thrilling and surreal experience.

government responded: trash trucks with plow blades appeared on the streets, sweeping them clean, and teams of city tow trucks and snow plows worked the streets — first the tow trucks cleared away the cars, then the snow plows eliminated the snow. Then the cars were returned to their spots. When the snow does come down, it is somewhat different in New York than elsewhere. Snow drifts on ledges at the thirty-fourth floor, icicles hang down unlikely lengths, and updrafts seize massive snowfalls and suddenly whisk them upward — atop the Empire State Building one can see snow fall upward. Drifts are torn away from roofs at a height of hundreds and hundreds feet above street level, scattering snow into the wind as if atop some Alpine peak. Most remarkable of all however is the winter in New York's parks. Cross-country skiing becomes exceedingly popular in Prospect Park in Brooklyn and in Manhattan's Central Park; when the various lakes freeze over, ice skating becomes equally widespread. Sledding abounds. The parks become magical in the snow — during one recent winter, Prospect Park, blanketed with snow, was covered with a haze that would have done justice to a Scottish glen; the slenderest branches and the stoutest trunks of all the trees bore a thick sleeve of glittering ice. The rivers too become receptacles for snow; huge dumpsters of the sweepings from the streets are tossed into the water of the East River and the Hudson, and bob away, melting and dissolving; there is, moreover, something eerie and moving about seeing snow fall upon — or into — the surface of a river, disappearing upon contact with the sullen grey stream. The image is completed when a snow-drift laden freighter pulls into view, to show that the white stuff is truly falling over the water as well as on land. Huge ice floes come sailing down the Hudson, and sometimes the entire vast river — technically a fjord and not a river at all, because it is subject to tidal ebbs and flows — freezes all the way over to the New Jersey shore. When the river breaks up, it is the strangest thing — you can see the great white chunks of ice bobbing downstream and, a few hours later, flowing upstream with the inrushing tide.

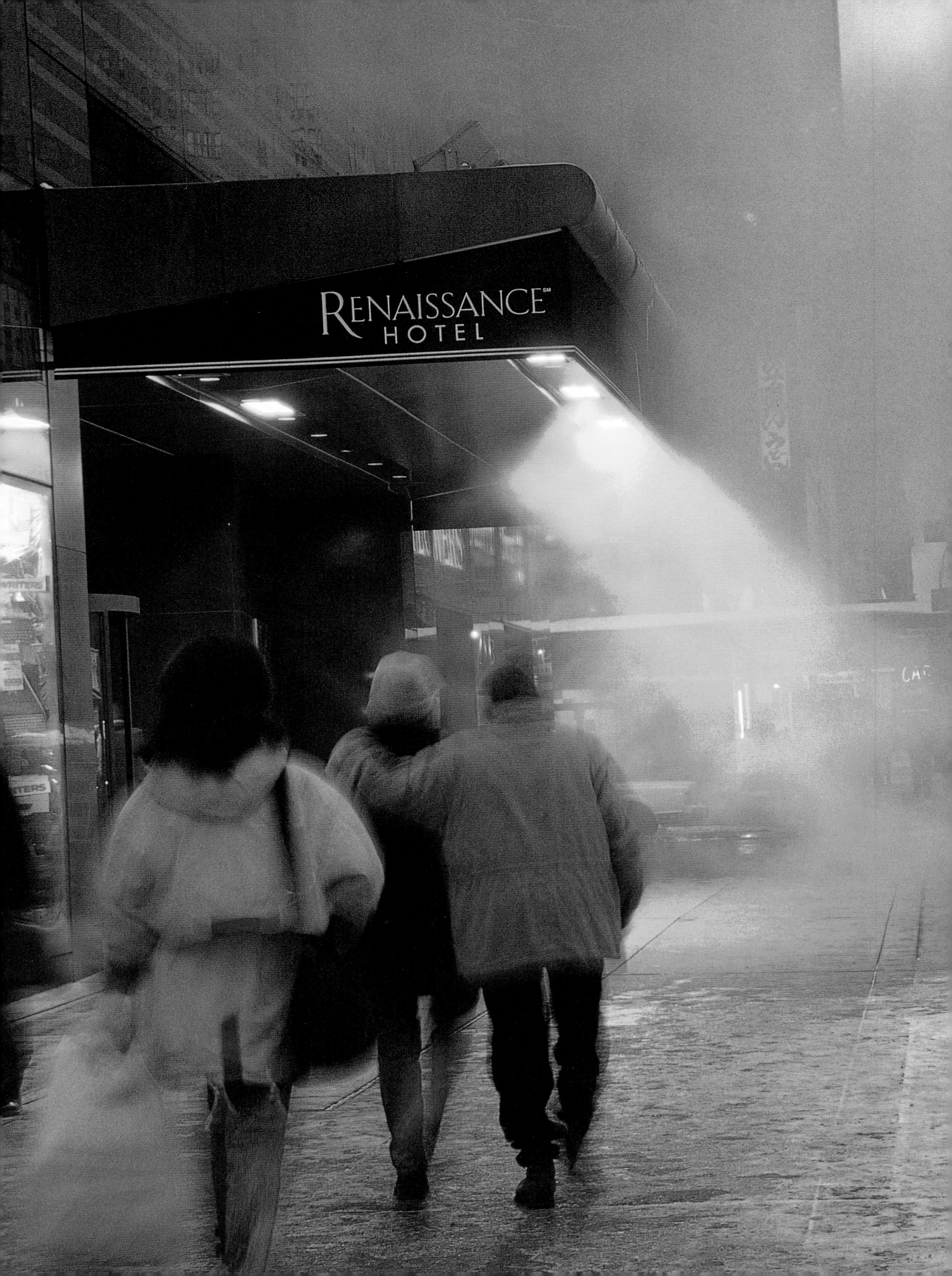
RENAISSANCE
HOTEL

108 top A spin through Central Park aboard a New York hansom cab is particularly evocative when the park is full of white drifts.

108-109 Snow is an architectural accessory in a city like New York. As lovely as Frank Lloyd Wright's Guggenheim Museum is normally, a powdering of snow gives a chilly beauty to its unusual round form.

109 top Dogwalkers do considerable business along Fifth Avenue, and when winter comes, lazy owners have all the more reasons to entrust Fido to a professional.

110-111 At the corner of Broadway and Seventh Avenue, Times Square is one of the most frantic places in New York; known as the "crossroads of the world," it boasts one of the greatest concentrations of movie houses, theaters, music stores, bars, art galleries, and porno emporiums in the Western world.

LIGHTS OF THE CITY

Riding the ferryboat back from the Statue of Liberty at sunset, at that crepuscular magic hour in which all things red seem to glow with an unearthly vibrance and power, one can witness a startling transformation in the massive promontory of skyscrapers that crowd the southern tip of the island. Many of the buildings down here have as much rock in their construction as they do steel and glass, and the softening failing light caresses the natural material of granite, brick, slate, and marble, eliciting an entrancing luminous pulse. As the ferryboat cuts through the choppy waves, Manhattan begins to look less and less like a part of the workaday world, and more and more like some strange outsized piece of elaborate medieval architecture. Let oneself slip into the strange revery that accompanies this sight, and soon — if the ferryboat ride has been perfectly timed — an even more amazing transition takes place: the soft ruddy hues of the sunset give way to the hard crystal and silver of nighttime on the Manhattan skyline, as the buildings begin to light up. A boat on the water, any of the bridges, or a high window will show the glittering vertical carpet of lights that all the city's skyscrapers present to the night sky. Of all the bridges, as we have noted elsewhere, the Brooklyn Bridge offers the most uncanny view — walking across its central pedestrian lane into lower Manhattan's uncanny kingdom of light is an unforgettable experience, especially because the luminous buildings amidst the darkness truly give some idea of their vast bulk as one draws near at a normal walking pace. From just about any place in Manhattan between Fourteenth Street and Fifty-Ninth Street, one of the landmarks one is most likely to see at night is the Empire State Building, lit up in various colors. The colors vary by season, and sometimes represent special occasions: when Columbia University holds its graduation ceremonies each year, for example, the school colors (blue and white) appear on the tip of the Empire State Building. Yellow, red, purple, green, and orange alternate through the year — laser shows have been used at various times to

112 This uncanny canyon of lights is lower Manhattan at nightfall. Although the sunlight is gone, the day is hardly over. In many of these lighted offices, people are still hard at work, while in all the rest the cleaning crew — ghostly denizens of the night — is already clearing up the wreckage from the day's activity.

113 The glittering spire of the Chrysler Building becomes even more magical and unearthly with the coming of night; completed in 1930, this building became the tallest in the world for only a few months, and then was outranked by the Empire State Building.

114 top Times Square is a kingdom of neon signs and uninhibited, tolerant lifestyles that are equally garish and flashy; it remains a major theater district as well, famous for its openings of shows that then tour the world.

114-115 Radio City Music Hall was originally an independent project, constructed on a license from Rockefeller Center. Its early years, however, were less than successful, the original investors declared bankruptcy, and the auditorium is now managed by the Center. Although all sorts of entertainers appear here, the popular imagination calls for the Rockettes, a Las Vegas-style chorus line.

115 top The Helmsley
Building, which is in turn
oppressed by the massive
bulk of the MetLife Building
— originally the PanAm
Building — looms over Park
Avenue.

emblazon images upon what is arguably the world's most famous skyscraper. One of the most remarkable things about sunsets and other nocturnal phenomena in Manhattan is that they appear intermittently along narrow canyons between skyscrapers. Thus, sunset over New Jersey appears as a gorgeous ruddy crescendo wedged into the narrow slots of the streets, and if you are walking along a north-south avenue, then the same sunset appears and reappears, as you cross street after street. The same is true of low-riding moons and planets, like a series of modern canvases; one wonders how much of an influence this may have had upon New York's artists. Other incredible sights in the New York night are the trees outside of Tavern-on-the-Green, at Central Park's southwest corner: some demented restaurateur decided that stringing Christmas lights on every tree in sight would make the gloomy night-time park somehow more cheerful — perhaps New Yorkers like it because the trees now look like so many skyscrapers. A more agreeable night-time sight in Central Park can be found further north: the Temple of Dendur, saved from the encroaching waters of the Nile south of the Aswan Dam in the late Sixties, was dismantled and shipped to New York's Metropolitan Museum of Art, and housed in a giant glass wing of the building — strollers in the evening are thus treated to a giant museum case, softly lit, with an ancient sandstone temple set out for public view. Along Fifth Avenue stands number 666, with its sinister address glowing redly high in the dark — the number of the Antichrist. The Citibank Building, at East Fifty-Ninth Street, is a perplexing sight by night or day, with its odd wedge-shaped crown. But on cold evenings, the wraithing wisps that emerge from its peak give it an odd and distrait beauty. There is, however, one last feature regarding the lights and darkness of Manhattan, that should be noted here, and it is a more general note than a specific site or address: at night, every single high point in Manhattan offers a different array of bright towers, silhouettes, and shadows. Going up to look at the city at night from a new vantage point is like turning a kaleidoscope for a new, unprecedented view of the city.

N*ew Yor*k

116-117 The delicate pinkish hues that envelop Central Park are not the result of a photographer's filter, but the work of one of New York's splendid sunsets.

118-119 The lights of nighttime festivities glow in Pier 17, overlooking the East River, at the foot of the skyscrapers of Lower Manattan. This pier was restored as part of the South Street Seaport Development Project.

120 top The facade of Henri Bendel on Fifth Avenue glows with discreet — and pricey — luxury. Fifth Avenue is the most important street on the East Side, and abounds in expensive residences, five-star hotels, luxury stores for blocks and blocks.

120-121 The statue of General Sherman faces one of the elegant statues surrounding Central Park.

121 This heroic statue of Mercury in triumph tops the facade of the Grand Central Terminal (although it is often called Grand Central Station, Terminal is the correct name, as this is the end of the line for all arriving trains). Perhaps Mercury is now triumphing at his own survival: this building was slated for demolition, until citywide protest ensured its preservation.

122-123 Times Square by night is a spectacle of neon and traffic — a new addition to one of the world's most famous intersections is the sign board over the Panasonic ad: it provides a running estimated count of the number of murders committed with guns in the United States.

124-125 Like giant glass prisms glittering with myriads of inner lights, the skyscrapers of Manhattan claw at the sky, in a dizzying perspective of intersecting straight lines.

126-127 Manhattan seen by night from the Brooklyn waterfront is a glorious spectacle of looming dark silhouettes and glittering lights and colors. The lovely lights conceal dark secrets — both in the dark waters of the East River and in the offices of Wall Street.

128 The towering mast of the Empire State Building was designed as a mooring mast for dirigibles: the Hindenberg disaster and the abandonment of dirigibles led to the mast quickly being used in a new technology — as a television and radio broadcasting antenna.

NEW YORK

PHOTO CREDITS